Turning Back the Pages on Nottinghamshire Ca

Canal and LMS Goods Station, 1927.

Compiled by Ray and Joanne Bickel

ISBN 978-0-902751-66-8

The Nottingham Canal - a brief history

On the 26th October 1790 a meeting of prominent businessmen, at the Guildhall, Nottingham, brought the Nottingham Canal into being. The Nottingham Corporation backed the plan, despite opposition from the existing Erewash Canal Company. This company only supported the building of the Beeston Cut which linked the River Trent with the new canal at Lenton. The Act for constructing the canal received Royal Assent on 1st January 1792. It would run from a junction with the Cromford Canal at Langley Mill, Derbyshire to a junction with the River Trent below Trent Bridge.

The engineer for the canal was William Jessop who surveyed the line in 1791. The first sod was cut in July 1792 and although it was open throughout by 1796, the canal was not officially completed until 1802. The cost of £80,000 was paid off by 1804 and the first dividend was paid to shareholders in the following year.

The canal had nineteen locks and one stop lock at Langley Mill and was 14 ¾ miles in length. It made a steep ascent from Lenton through to Wollaton in a series of fourteen locks over 2 ¾ miles. Originally thirty-four bridges were built, twenty-seven were of masonry stone or red brick, four were swing bridges and two were red brick with timber tops.

The main cargoes were coal from the various collieries along the canal, iron, stone, limestone, manure and a small amount of farm produce. Receipts on the canal built up from the 1800s to reach a record £12,825 19s 10d in 1839. However this was the year the first railway reached Nottingham and by 1844 receipts had declined to under £10,000 per year. The company finally sold out to the Ambergate and Manchester Railway in 1855. By the 1900s most of the trade on the canal was to the wharves in the centre of Nottingham while the collieries at Radford and Wollaton had a small amount of trade. Receipts had collapsed by 1916 to £1,028.

By 1928 the Nottingham Canal was in bad repair. It was very neglected and traffic ceased above Lenton in 1928 with official abandonment in 1937. Further deterioration occurred until 1966 when, prompted by complaints from nearby housing of frequent flooding, the canal was drained and piped from Derby Road, Lenton to Trowell.

Today the Nottingham Canal is intact from Meadow Lane Lock to Lenton where it joins the Beeston Cut. The navigable route runs through the Beeston Cut to rejoin the River Trent. Redevelopment of the adjacent land has been intense. The industrial area of Boots Island and the Poplar Cut have been transformed into leisure and service developments while the Wilford Street area now houses a variety of users from the Inland Revenue and the Evening Post to a lively nightbar area. Meanwhile high up in Awsworth and Cossall the canal is used for fishing although a significant part of it has vanished under opencast mining developments.

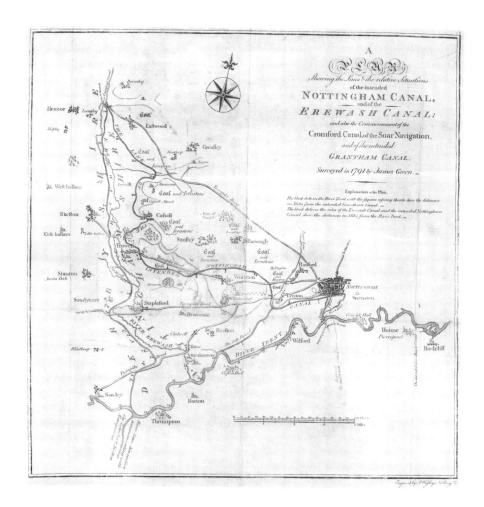

Nottingham and Erewash Canal, 1791. A portion of the plan surveyed in 1791 by James Green shows the 'intended line' of the Nottingham Canal. Parliamentary approval of the Cromford Canal in 1789 brought fears that distant collieries would send their coal to Nottingham at the expense of local coal mines. This gave a head of steam to the proponents of the Nottingham Canal. *(NTGM017917)*

Junction of the Cromford, Nottingham and Erewash canals at Derby Road Langley Mill, c.1955. The small building to the right of centre is a gauging house. Beside it is the toll house used by both the Nottingham and Cromford canal companies. The water supply for the Nottingham canal at this point was from the Moorgreen reservoir a couple of miles away towards Hucknall.
Image credit: R. G. Hughes (DMAG000539)

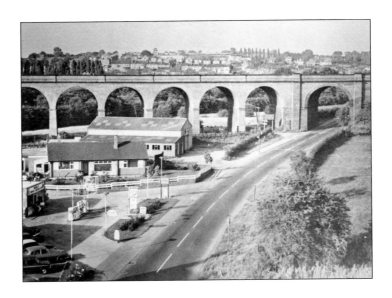

Giltbrook Viaduct, c.1960. Above the Nottingham canal at Giltbrook is the 'Forty Bridges' of the Great Northern Awsworth to Pinxton line. The line was built to exploit the coal measures of the Erewash Valley. The viaduct bridged the Giltbrook, the Ilkeston to Kimberley Road, shown here, and included two skew spans across ground level railways. The viaduct had thirty nine arches, two of which were blocked to form stone buildings. It was demolished in 1973. *(NCCC002480)*

Nottingham Canal, Awsworth, 1975. The canal is crossed by the disused Great Northern Railway Line at Awsworth in 1975. In the water can be seen the remains of a coal carrying "butty" barge. This area supported the shallow mines of Awsworth, Shilo and Bennerley Collieries. The remains of these mines and much of the canal were swallowed up by opencast mining seen here to the left of the towpath. The small red brick bridge supported with iron braces and the railway bridge have both disappeared. Just 50 yards to the left of the photograph is an amazing survivor, the wrought iron Bennerley Viaduct, a ¼ mile long with sixteen spans standing 52 feet above the Erewash Valley. *Image credit: Reg Baker (NTGM006953)*

The canal near Awsworth, 1976. Located about 100 yards south of Newtons Lane, this photograph shows the remains of two types of barges which have lain there since the closure of the canal. The larger one was a coal carrying 'butty' barge and bears a number near the bow. The smaller one would have been used by the maintenance staff of the canal company for various installations. *Image credit: Reg Baker (NTGM017927)*

Wrought iron bridge west of Cossall village, 1976. This bridge is the remains of the old Cossall Colliery Drift. The colliery closed in 1966 and the old slag heap developed a brief new life as a ski slope. The view from the top reveals the canal to have formed a letter U as it followed the contours of the area. *Image credit: Reg Baker (NTGM017926)*

Mill Lane, Cossall, 1966. This is a swing bridge of the type now restored at Langley Mill basin. In the background is the slag heap of Cossall Colliery. When Oakwood Colliery closed in 1957 the workforce was transferred to nearby Cossall. The Erewash Canal is in the valley about 1 mile away.
Image credit: Guardian Journal, Nottingham Evening Post (NTGM008223)

Looking west towards the M1 motorway, 1976. This stretch of the motorway was opened in 1966 and breaches the canal which was piped underneath. This section of the canal was bought in 1977 by Broxtowe Borough Council. Restoration work began in 1984 in collaboration with a number of interested organisations. Work has continued over the years but due to problems on the route the complete return to water had to be ruled out and some infilling has taken place. *Image credit: Reg Baker (NTGM006954)*

The Nottingham Canal, off Coventry Lane near Balloon Woods, Bramcote, c.1900. The road bridge shown has now become the busy A6002. The canal has been filled in until it joins with the Beeston Cut. There are numerous signs of its former existence along the route. *Image credit: A P Knighton (DCHQ500693)*

Canal Lock and Wollaton Colliery, 1966. The houses on the left are on Welwyn Road, those on the right are on Bridge Road. The Wollaton area saw the first wooden railway in England. It was built in 1604 to transport coal to the population of Nottingham. The coal would have been dug from bell pits. The Wollaton Colliery deep pit was opened in 1874 and closed at the end of 1963 though it remained open for nine months to remove the machinery. The canal itself was drained on the 29th August 1966. It is now buried under Torvill Drive. *Image credit: G.L. Roberts (NTGM012446)*

Canal Lock 10 looking towards Lock 11, 1953.

Locks 9, 10 and 11 were very close together and formed a flight.

On the flight was a plethora of typical canal buildings including a blacksmiths, bricklayers, carpenters, and a timber store. The canal workshops were also here. Boats and lock gates were repaired at the workshops.

Also on the flight was a wharf where lime was loaded from nearby kilns. At Woodyard Lane there was a timber mill which specialised in making pit props. These were then delivered via the canal. *Image credit: City Engineers Department (NTGM006956)*

Houses on Charlbery Road line the banks of the canal. It was near here in 1940, during an air raid on Nottingham by a lone bomber, that some houses were destroyed and people were killed. The target of this raid, which was missed, was in fact the railway line.

The infilling of this section began in 1955 and was completed by 1962 when the locks were removed. *Image credit: City Engineers Department (NTGM006957)*

Canal Lock 6, 1925. This was situated just before the Radford Bridge, now the Nottingham Outer Ring Road. Originally the entrance to the lock was close to the bridge. When the road was widened the lock was filled in but it is still visible from the new underpass. *Image credit: F.W. Stevenson (NTGM006889)*

Canal Lock 4, c.1895. This lock was situated close to Lenton Lodge. The old Wollaton park gate was the entrance to the park grounds until 1925 when Nottingham Corporation purchased the land to build houses. The wall of the park can be seen in the photograph to the left and is where the A52 passes over. The old canal bridge can still be seen at this point. *Image credit: A.W. Bird (NTGM009883)*

Bridge 9 with Lenton Lodge to left, 1928. The barge in the photograph was in operation in 1937, the last year of usage of this section of the canal. Although Wollaton Hall is Elizabethan, Lenton Lodge was built in 1824 with twenty eight rooms. At the time, the Luddites were extremely active and the Middleton family were afraid they may be attacked. So they incorporated a winching mechanism which allowed the gates to open and close quickly from the inside. It is still there, but is no longer functional. As the gatehouse, it was designed for occupation by servants, but sometimes hunting parties would get drunk and stay overnight. The 7th Lord Middleton apparently kept a mistress there. *Image credit: F.W. Stevenson (NTGM006955)*

The lodge was designed by Sir Jeffry Wyatville, also known as Wyatt, and was built 1823-5. It is separated from Wollaton Park by suburban housing built in the 1920s. The lodge was allowed to decay until 1981 when an interior designer, Lawrie Williamson, carried out an extensive renovation. The lodge features four round towers. Staircases in the rear towers open onto a lead roof. From here views of Wollaton Hall can be obtained.

Lenton Boatyard, 1850. The boatyard opened in 1796 and was taken over by Thomas Trevethick in 1903. He moved the firm from Gainsborough after being persuaded this spot was better for commercial trade. The buildings on the right became the Midland Orphanage and Industrial Training Institution for Girls in 1863. Closing in 1922, the building was bought by Crepe Sizes Limited and was converted into premises for the production of elastic yarn. The firm gradually knocked down the buildings and built new ones. These have now been demolished with housing occupying the site. *Image credit: T.C. Moore, Nottingham City Council (NTGM009589)*

Clayton's Bridge, 1910. In the background a church can be seen through the arch of the bridge. Nearby was the medieval Lenton Priory founded in the early 12th Century and dissolved in 1538. It was one of only six Cluniac priories founded in this country and was the most important in Nottinghamshire. Only one pillar is preserved above ground level in the area. *Image credit: G.A. Sewell (NTGM006928)*

'Francesca', Trevithicks Pleasure Steamer, 1905. Thomas Trevithick took over two coal fired pleasure steamers when he occupied the boatyard in 1903. Every Thursday and Sunday these made trips down to Trent Lock and back for 1s 3d until the First World War. Trips further afield could also be booked. Normanton on Soar and Shardlow were popular trips. Sometimes trailer boats were attached and up to two hundred people could travel. *Image credit: Lenton Local History Group (NTGM017923)*

Lenton Boatyard, 1929. In the background is the Gregory Street Bridge which was replaced by the Lenton Lane Road Bridge. The navigable section links with the

Beeston Cut and now sees a lot of leisure craft like the boat shown on the left. Note the skyline of Nottingham in the background. *Image credit: F.W. Stevenson (NTGM006924)*

A sailing boat in the Park Wharf, 1885. The Castle Boulevard was built in the 1890s. Prior to this it was a semi rural lane which had wharves, dry docks, workshops and boat yards. *Image credit: T.C. Moore, Nottingham City Council (NTGM007094)*

Sailing barge at Duke's Wharves underneath Nottingham Castle, 1860. Three wharves were built at right angles to the canal. The Duke was the Duke of Newcastle whose family had acquired the lease to the castle in 1641. The ruins were cleared in 1663 and the first Duke's palace completed in 1673. It was attacked in 1831 by reform rioters but was restored in 1878 and now houses a number of museums. The wharves themselves were filled in 1884 for the building of Castle Boulevard. *Image credit: Nottingham Historical Film Unit (NTGM006925)*

Castle Lock, c.1950. This is Lock 2, Lock 1 being Trent Lock which is still in operation. The lock is capable of taking barges up to 14 feet in width. The scene is dominated by Viyella House the classic 'art nouveau' building of the headquarters of William Hollins and Co. Ltd. Designed in 1930 by Frank Broadhead in a reinforced concrete design it was sold by William Hollis in the early 1960s and redesigned by Bendigo Properties as its headquarters. The refurbished warehouse to the left was built in 1894. *Image credit: J. Orton (NTGM017929)*

Wilford Street, Road Bridge, c1950. This is a wrought iron bridge standing 9 feet 5 inches above the canal with a span of 36 feet. Directly underneath is the Canal Lock. Major redevelopment has seen the offices of the Nottingham Evening Post relocated to the area on the right of the shot. *(NTGM017938)*

Canal near Navigation Inn, 1882. This painting shows the original Navigation Inn built in 1787. It was the terminus of passenger barges which ran to Cromford and Leicester. In the foreground is the overflow leading into the Tinker's Leen.
Image credit: T.C. Moore, Nottingham City Council (NTGM006926)

Trent Navigation Warehouse, c.1930. This pre First World War warehouse had two large doors on each floor and had hoists to unload goods from barges on the canal. The building was converted in 1998-2000 to house Jongleurs Comedy Club, a health club and a Wetherspoon's pub. In the foreground is the Earle's cement depot. They were based in Hull and operated from 1811 to 1954. *(NTGM017937)*

Fellows, Clayton and Morton Wharf and Warehouse, c.1920. The wharf is a four storey red brick warehouse with two Victorian hand cranes in front. The Fellows, Morton and Clayton company were a canal carrying company based in Birmingham. They ran a network of fast barges or flys which worked day and night. By 1915 the steamer barges were replaced by diesel. The company was finally wound up in 1948 and taken over by British Waterways. *(NTGM017935)*

Looking towards Carrington Street, 1894. The original Carrington Street Bridge was designed by Mr. Moses Wood and was erected by Messrs. Court & Company. It cost in the region of £6,000 and provided a direct link for the Midland Railway from its station to central Nottingham. It was of such importance to the railway company that the directors of the Midland Railway paid half the cost. As traffic increased it was widened into its present form in 1902. *Image credit: A. Johnson. (NTGM009590)*

Carrington Street Bridge, c.1960. Showing the later Carrington Road bridge of 1902 with its attractive rosette panelled steel balustrades built by the Butterley Iron Co. for £4,550 15s. On the immediate left can be seen the Fellows, Clayton and Morton wharf.

In 1818 a tragic accident occurred when a boatman dropped a hot clinker onto a leaking store of gunpowder. The ensuing explosion killed eight men and two boys. It was said a boatman was flung 100 yards across to the other side of the canal. *(NTMG017936)*

East from Trent Street Bridge, c.1950. The canal is crossed here by the former Great Northern line from Trent Lane to Weekday Cross. This section was built by Nowell and Sons at the cost of £109,940 5s 3d in July 1896. It was part of a complicated section of the canal which was also crossed by the former Great Central Railway.

Both lines joined at Weekday Cross and ran into the joint owned Victoria Station. Closed in 1966 this is now the Victoria Shopping Centre. The Great Northern line is still evident but the bridge over the canal has been removed. *Image credit: J. Orton. (NTGM017928)*

Bridge over Nottingham Canal at Trent Street, 1965. The bridge has been demolished to be replaced as part of a traffic experiment. Just at the far left is the viaduct of the Great Central Railway and the signal box at Weekday Cross.

Part of this viaduct is now in use for the tram line which ends at Station Street. The neo-gothic Unitarian chapel erected in 1876 can be seen in the background. It was recently converted into the stylish Pitcher and Piano bar and restaurant.
Image credit: Guardian Journal, Nottingham Evening Post (NTGM017920)

Taken from the Great Northern Line Bridge, 1975. View of the early 19th Century timber wharves at the rear of Canal Street. To the left is the Trevitt's Building damaged by German bombing in the Second World War.

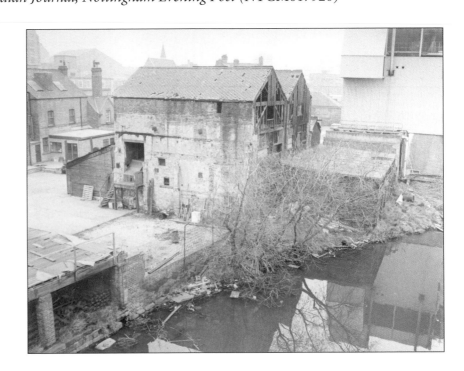

Just to the right is the former Ice Stadium which was demolished in 1999 after a sixty year history. Next along to the right is the spire of St Patrick's Roman Catholic Church.
Image credit: Reg Baker (NTGM017921)

The Poplar Arm of the Nottingham Canal, c.1900. Situated on the viaduct to the right of the painting is the London and North Eastern Railway line and 'High Level Station'. This was closed in 1967 and was recently demolished to free land for commercial development. The Poplar Arm joined and followed the old course of the River Leen which was navigable to the Broadmarsh Wharves. *Image credit: Annie Gilbert, reproduced with kind permission from a private collection (NTGM017941)*

Painting of Fothergill's Basin, Poplar Arm, Sneinton, 1885. This is the stretch of the Poplar Arm that was extended by Earl Manvers of Thoresby in 1836 towards the Hermitage in the background. Not only did this allow for further access, but also additional mooring. It was infilled later to allow for the building of Manvers Street. *Image credit: T.C. Moore, Nottingham City Council (NTGM006888)*

Nottingham from Flood Road, approaching the toll gate on London Road, 1808. There was once a mile of marshes and flood plain between the city of Nottingham and the river at Trent Bridge. Up to the 18th century these were common lands criss-crossed by the channels of the River Leen. A series of wooden bridges were replaced c.1766 by stone structures and by 1790 a single ten arch bridge was erected. It was badly maintained, and in 1795 it had to be pulled down after flood damage. In the following year an Act of Parliament established a Turnpike Trust for the route from the north side of Trent Bridge to the west of St. Mary's Church. The new turnpike ran alongside the new Nottingham canal and crossed the Meadows on arches that enabled the floodwater to drain away. Traces of some remain today. The road was a great success. With the owners investing the income on upkeep, and competing to draw traffic from the canal, it was well maintained and busy. It became a favourite promenade from Nottingham. It is not known exactly when the tolls were done away with, but they certainly lasted until 1860. Three churches of Nottingham can be seen. From left to right they are St Nicholas, St Peter and St Mary.
Image credit: Unknown Artist, Nottingham City Council (NTGM017934)

Meadow Lane Bridge, 1973. The original Bridge 1 is a stone structure. The towpath is on the left hand side having crossed on a change-over bridge just after the Poplar Arm. The boats would normally have been moored at the Turney Brothers Leatherworks which can be seen in the background. *Image credit: Reg Baker (NTGM017933)*

The River Trent with Meadow Lane Lock, 1973. The quay and lock keepers house can be seen in front of the leatherworks, now replaced by a housing development. The leatherworks themselves had replaced an old dock that was filled in 1861. The lock unusually has handles fitted to the gearing rather than using a windlass. *Image credit: Reg Baker (NTGM017916)*

The Beeston Cut - a brief history

The Beeston Cut was part of the original Act of Parliament for the Nottingham Canal but the branch was dropped. However, following a joint appeal from the Erewash Canal and Trent Navigation Companies, agreement was reached to share the cost of construction. Parliamentary approval followed in 1794 with completion in 1796. The engineer was John Bailey and the branch cost £6,141. The cut had just two locks: the entrance from the River Trent and one to its right which was used for boats with a shallow draft. This entrance is now blocked off and the gates have gone. It is fed by water from the River Trent and has five bridges two of which are originals. The cut became fairly busy with traffic coming from the Erewash and Derby canals and long distance traffic from the Trent and Mersey and Grand Union canals. However trade declined, largely due to the poor maintenance of the Nottingham wharves. In 1936 the Trent Navigation Company added the last two miles of the Nottingham canal to the Beeston Cut which in recent years has become very popular with leisure users.

Original pedestrian bridge on the Beeston Cut, 1973. This bridge, called Chain Lane, took pedestrians from Gibbons Street to Redfield Way in the Dunkirk area of the city. The main line railway from Nottingham to Trent Junction, the A52 Nottingham outer bypass and a bowling alley, multiplex cinema and a nightclub are all near this junction with the former branch. *Image credit: Reg Baker (NTGM006942)*

Beeston Lock, View from the west gate of the lock, 1973. This is the lock at the western end of the canal which links it with the River Trent. The footbridge is over the main Beeston Lock. The second lock can be seen to the right of the photograph with two moored craft in the entrance. The cut originally had eight gates, now all removed.
Image credit: Reg Baker (NTGM006949)

Beeston Lock seen from the River Trent. In the foreground a leisure boat is moored at Beeston Marina on the River Trent. In the background can be seen Beeston Lock and the lock keeper's cottage at the start of the Beeston Cut. *(NCCS001937)*

Beeston Lock, c.1970. The main river lock is shown here on the right. The second lock on the left, linked to the River Trent. It had flood gates fixed at the river end to stop water flowing back into the canal in times of river flood.
Image credit: Nottingham Weekly Guardian, Nottingham Evening Post (NTGM006948)

The Grantham Canal - a brief history

The Grantham Canal was born out of the desire to transport goods, especially coal, cheaply. Originally presented to Parliament in 1792 the bill was thrown out. However, on 30th April the following year consent was obtained. The Act was for a 33 mile canal from Radcliffe to Grantham, later changed to West Bridgford, with a 3½ mile branch from Cropwell Butler to Bingham which was never built. The construction work was divided between two engineers, James Green for Nottinghamshire and William King for the rest. The fall from Grantham to the Trent is approximately 140 feet. The first traffic was on the eastern end of the canal and the first load was carried in April 1797. There were some problems near Cropwell Bishop due to the gypsum mineral beds encountered there, but the canal was opened throughout by the summer. The canal shipped coal, coke, lime, building materials and groceries from Nottingham to the various villages on the canal and to Grantham. Agricultural produce from Lincolnshire was transported in the opposite direction. Trade grew to a profit in 1820, reached a peak in 1839 and continued to make money until the opening of the Nottingham to Grantham railway in 1851.

Within three years the railway acquired the canal and trade steadily declined up till the end of the century. During the First World War the canal was used for transporting stores and men. In 1929, with trade almost at a standstill, the owners, 'London and North Eastern Railway', closed it. Legally abandoned in 1936 the canal was largely maintained in water due to agreements to support agricultural interests. This was done even though eighteen of the road bridges along the route needed to be replaced. In 1969 the Grantham Canal Society was formed with the aim of restoring the majority of the original canal into full working order. Two unsuccessful funding bids were made: £12 million to the Millennium Fund and £25 million to the Big Lottery Fund for a new link to the River Trent using the former Cotgrave mineral line's formation. Over the past fifteen years £6 million of work has been funded by grants raised by the Society. This has brought some of the sections of the old canal back into full water.

George Pearson's narrow boat 'Fred' on the Grantham Canal, 1895 p. 25.
The boat can be seen entering the canal from the River Trent at West Bridgford. George Pearson was a barge owner and coal dealer in Victorian times. He lodged at the beer house kept by Benjamin Wright at Woolsthorpe Wharf in Lincolnshire.
Image credit: T.C. Moore (NTGM007097)

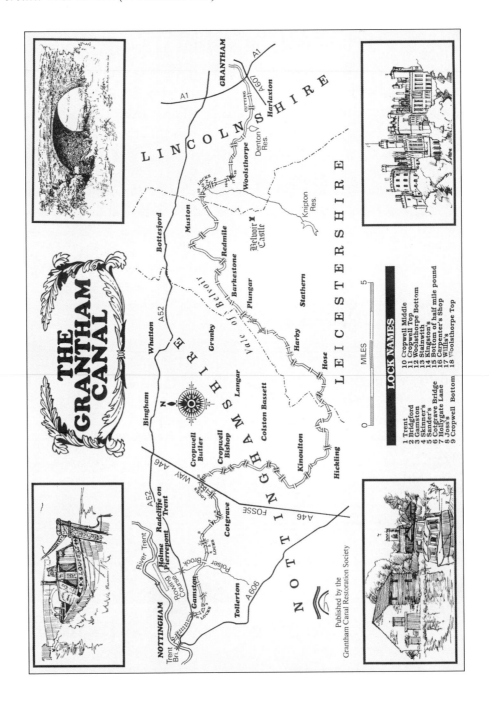

LOCK NAMES

1 Trent
2 Bridgford
3 Gamston
4 Skinner's
5 Sander's
6 Cotgrave Bridge
7 Hollygate Lane
8 Joss's
9 Cropwell Bottom
10 Cropwell Middle
11 Cropwell Top
12 Woolsthorpe Bottom
13 Stainwith
14 Kingston's
15 Bottom of half mile pound
16 Carpenter's Shop
17 Willis's
18 Woolsthorpe Top

The Grantham Canal, 1992. From the East Midlands Yearbook of the Institution of Civil Engineers. The map shows the canal's progress from the River Trent through three counties to the town of Grantham. *Image credit: Grantham Canal Society*

Lock No 1, Sept 1961.

It was known as Trent Lock because it fed into the River Trent. This lock was restored first by the Trent River Authority and later by the Grantham Canal Restoration Society.

The gates were permanently sealed by Severn Trent Water to prevent flooding. In the background can be seen the old stands of Nottingham Forest Football Club and Trent Bridge at the extreme right. *Image credit: G.L. Roberts (NTGM007081)*

Lady Bay Railway Bridge, a stop girder bridge, c.1922. There is some confusion about Lady Bay Bridge. It appears that the first Lady Bay Bridge was a bridge over the Bridgford Brook in 1320. The bridge was named after the Virgin Mary who had a chapel nearby. When the Nottingham to Melton Mowbray railway line was built the Trent railway crossing became Bridge 2 while this, Bridge 4, was called Lady Bay. After the demolition of Bridge 4, Bridge 2 was renamed Lady Bay Bridge when it was converted to take road vehicles in 1979. *Image credit: Nottingham City Council (NTGM007079)*

Boys fishing under Lady Bay Bridge, 1952. The railway from Nottingham to Melton Mowbray was built by the Midland Railway as an alternative route to London and to open up a route south east of Nottingham.

Built by Arid and Sons from 1875 the railway opened to Goods and Minerals in 1879 and to passengers in 1880. *Image credit: Eric Lee (NCCS000317)*

Passenger train on Lady Bay Railway Bridge, 3rd Aug 1953. No station was provided at West Bridgford which at the time of the opening of the line was only a small village. However as it grew it is perhaps surprising that no later station was built. *(NCCS001811)*

Lady Bay Railway Bridge, 1974. This photo was taken after the closure of the line in 1967 and looks south. Part of the line from Plumtree to the junction near Melton Mowbray is retained as a track for railway testing. Trent Boulevard can be seen to the left while to the right is Radcliffe Road. The bridge is measured at 122 miles 46 chains  from London by rail and is now occupied by the Lady Bay Workshops. *Image credit: Reg Baker (NTGM017918)*

Lady Bay Railway Bridge, 1975. This photo was taken from the site of the Lady Bay Bridge. Seen through the bridge is Orston Road East, the location for Severn Trent Water's maintenance yard. On the right is the Boots Lady Bay Sportsground. *Image credit: Reg Baker (NTGM007078)*

Lady Bay Road Bridge, c.1816. The artist, William Frederick Austini, depicts the canal in its heyday. The canal is now culverted and is the line for the new by-pass which links the A52 with the former Trent Crossing now Lady Bay Bridge.
Image credit: Nottingham City Council (NTGM009207)

Lady Bay Road Bridge, 1960. Showing Bridge 2 which was finally demolished in 1961. The canal is now sited under a complex road junction in West Bridgford making restoration here highly unlikely. *Image credit: G.L. Roberts (NTGM017925)*

Bridge 3, the lifting bascule bridge in West Bridgford, c.1953, shortly before demolition. The bridge linked Radcliffe Road to Rutland Road. Bascule is a French term for seesaw and balance and bascule bridges operate along the same principle. They are the most common type of movable bridge because they open quickly and require relatively little energy to operate. *Image credit: T.W. Wyncoll (NTGM017924)*

Bridge 3a footbridge, c.1950. This footbridge is seen facing Gertrude Road and was locally known as the 'Meccano Bridge'. It linked Radcliffe Road, Rutland Road and Gertrude Street. As can be seen the canal has already been filled in and the footbridge is being demolished. *(NCCS001057)*

Schoolgroup on the frozen Grantham Canal with Rutland Road in the background, c.1950. At this point the canal runs for under a mile north of Radcliffe Road in West Bridgford. The canal would discharge water overfeeding from the Trent Lock into an overspill into the River Trent. *Image credit: F.W. Stevenson. (NTGM006668)*

Radcliffe Road, c.1950. Radcliffe Road appears to be a lot less busy than it is nowadays. The houses on the left hand side are Rutland Road in West Bridgford. The canal is still in good water at this point but its main use is for fishing as shown in the middle distance. *Image credit: Eric Lee (NCCS000528)*

Westbound Bridge carrying the A52 at Gamston, 1975. This is Bridge 4. The eastbound carriageway of the A52 can be seen through the bridge. The canal was piped under it through two concrete pipes. In the foreground is a wide section of the canal where barges had to wait as the bridge could only take one boat at a time. *Image credit: Reg Baker (NTGM07080)*

Clark's Bridge, Gamston, c.1905. This was Bridge 5 from the Trent junction and was a movable bridge like most of the farm access bridges on the canal. It has now been replaced by a flat pre-stressed concrete bridge.
Image credit: Nottingham City Council (NTGM009840)

Skinners Lock, 1960. This is Lock 11 and is currently degated. The water feeder is a diversion of the Polser Brook which flows through Cotgrave. *Image credit: Mr. Headland (West Bridgford Library 1451)*

Skinners Lock, 1960. A more distant view of the lock with Skinners Lock Cottage on the right hand side. The signs of neglect are only too obvious here. Nearby is the former Cotgrave Colliery which was built in the 1950s as one of the later National Coal Board deep mines. *Image credit: Mr. Headland (West Bridgford Library 1448)*

East Side of Fosse Way Bridge, 1960. This is one of a very few of the original remaining bridges from the 1790s. The west side of this bridge has been extended using blue bricks while this side of the bridge is in the original red brick of the canal builders. Near to here the canal has three locks known as the Cropwell Flight. *Image credit: Mr. Headland (West Bridgford Library 1452)*

The Canal, Cropwell Bishop, c.1930. After reaching the twenty mile pound just past the Fosse Bridge the canal is lock free until it reaches Woolsthorpe Bottom in Lincolnshire only six miles from Grantham. At this point the canal is approximately 150 feet above sea level. *Image credit: Nottingham City Council (NTGM017919)*

Canal Scene, Cropwell-Bishop.

Canal Scene, Cropwell Bishop, c.1960. A swan meanders along the canal in this peaceful postcard. In the vicinity was the proposed branch to Bingham which was never built. The branch would have terminated quarter of a mile south of Bingham. *Image credit: A.W. Bourne (NTGM017940)*

Cropwell Bishop, Town End, c.1930. This is probably Bridge 21 known as Town Bridge. It was demolished in 1948 and replaced by a two piped culvert. In this area the canal is now 'dry'. We have left behind the coal mining area and entered the gypsum beds. *(NCCS002038)*

Cropwell Bishop, The Old Humpback, c.1930. Postcard of the Town Bridge at a time when the canal was well watered. The engineers had problems sealing the canal bed because the canal runs through a gypsum seam. This is why the canal is currently dry. *Image credit: Copy of a 1930 postcard by Reg Baker (NCCS000187)*

Canal South of Cropwell Bishop. After the canal was abandoned a temporary dam was constructed at Spencer's Bridge, Bridge 24. This was to prevent the loss of water from the rest of the canal. The act of abandonment contained a clause that a minimum of 2 feet of water should be retained in the canal for agricultural purposes. This appears to have been adhered to as the canal from here to Grantham is in water.
Image credit: G.L. Roberts (NTGM007090)

Swing Bridge, Kinoulton, c.1910. Another of the distinctive swing bridges of the Grantham Canal, now replaced by a low concrete structure. The bridge has been opened to allow a boat passage along the canal although it is suspected this was 'posed' specifically for the postcard. *(NCCS002031)*

Ice Carnival, Kinoulton, 5th Feb 1917. The carnival is taking place on the waters of the canal. February 1917 was the coldest month of the First World War. There were some severe frosts in the first three weeks of the month, reaching -20C at Benson, Oxfordshire on the 6th. *(NCCS002037)*

The Bridge, Hickling, c.1900. This image is probably Bridge 30 in the village of Hickling. The basin in the foreground is now a major feature of the restored section of the Grantham Canal. Unfortunately the bridge here has been lowered and would cause problems for complete restoration. The canal is navigable, meandering for two further miles until it exits Nottinghamshire. *(NTGM017922)*

The Chesterfield Canal - a brief history

The building of the Chesterfield Canal dates from the first canal building boom and significantly predates both the Nottingham and Grantham Canals. The main originators of the canal were the traders of Chesterfield, East Derbyshire and South Yorkshire, who took their coal, lead and iron on roads to the River Trent at Bawtry. Although James Brindley was asked to determine a route for the canal, the initial survey was carried out by James Varley in 1769. Brindley estimated £100,000 would be needed to build the canal. However, after this initial survey, the towns of Worksop and Retford wanted the canal to pass through their towns. A new route was surveyed and a year later the Act was passed to build the canal from Chesterfield to the River Trent at West Stockwith. Work began in October 1771 at Norwood Tunnel. It took four years to build. Construction was going well when James Brindley died in September 1772 and the Clerk of the Works, John Varley, took over as Superintendent Engineer. However, by 1774, Hugh Henshall, Brindley's brother in law took charge and discovered that some of the work at the tunnel had been carried out poorly.

Originally the canal was to have been wide throughout but to save money the 'new route' was surveyed as narrow. In May 1775 the town of Retford paid for the canal to be wide enough to take Trent barges, 14 feet 6 inches, up to their town. However, it was only wide enough for narrow barges, 6 feet 11 inches, from Retford through to Chesterfield. In April 1776 the canal was opened from West Stockwith to Killamarsh just west of Norwood Tunnel and on June 4th 1777 the whole canal officially opened. It had cost £150,000 to build and unfortunately coincided with a national recession as a result of the American War of Independence. The first dividend of 1% was finally paid in 1789. By 1795 with the addition of some tramways linking the mines to the canal the dividend had risen to 6%.

The canal was not a through route, so was never very successful. In the early 1800s there was speculation it might extend into Sheffield but this never materialised. By 1844 competition arrived when Manchester, Sheffield and Lincolnshire Company proposed that a railway should be built from Sheffield to Gainsborough. Initially this was to have been built over the canal but after the railway company took over the running of the canal they built a line close to it instead. Surprisingly trade increased on the canal for a while despite the competition.

Throughout its history, problems were encountered at Norwood Tunnel. In the late 1800s £21,000 was spent repairing the tunnel as a result of subsidence caused by coal mining both above and underneath the bore. By 1904 the headroom of the tunnel was a mere 4 feet 10 inches and very few boats braved the journey. In 1907 a further fall directly under the road from Harthill to Kiveton Park closed the canal from the Chesterfield direction. Traffic had been minimal for many years and west of the colliery basin at Shireoaks the canal was abandoned.

The remainder of the canal was kept in fairly good condition and until 1955 bricks were regularly transported from the brick works at Walkeringham. After 1962 commercial traffic on the canal ceased and the eastern end was retained for leisure use. Things stagnated for many years and much of the western section was filled in. In 1976 the Chesterfield Canal Society was formed to restore the complete waterway. The first lock to reopen was at Tapton, very close to Chesterfield in 1990.

A £4.5 million plan to restore the disused section from Worksop to Shireoaks Colliery was largely financed by British Coal. It was used to redevelop the colliery basin for housing and boat mooring. The restoration of eight locks and three culverted bridges means the canal is navigable from the River Trent to the east portal of Norwood Tunnel. All the sections in Nottinghamshire can now be used.

River, lock and Edwin Gordon's boat at West Stockwith, c.1920. The boat is seen in the canal's terminal basin. This became the busiest part of the village when regular services began along the canal, but declined again when the canal lost its trade. *Image credit: Edwin Gordon, M. Payne (NTGM017939)*

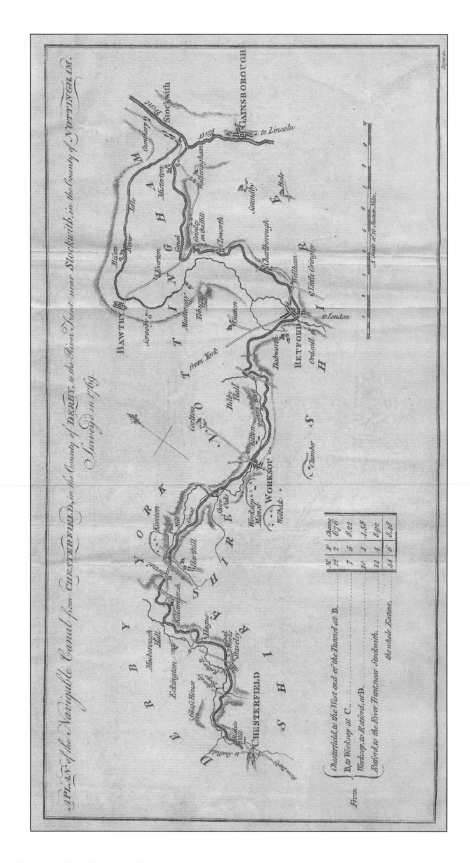

The Chesterfield Canal, 1769 *Image credit: Worksop Library Ephemera Collection*

Looking towards the Chesterfield Canal at West Stockwith, 1989. In the 14th century West Stockwith was very prosperous. The Trent riverbank was lined with warehouses, boat building yards and other associated trades. The remains of that prosperity can be seen in the houses on the banks. The church was built in the 18th century with money left by William Huntingdon, a ship's carpenter, on land that was formerly his boat building yard. *Image credit: Ian Brown (NCCN000289)*

Lock keeper's cottage at Gringley on the Hill, 1989. This is Gringley Top Lock which was maintained for thirty four years by William Antcliffe. He was known for his rule of iron in the section under his care.

The wharf near here had two working boats in the canal's heyday. *Image credit: Ian Brown (NTGM016850)*

Aerial photo of canal at Gringley on the Hill, c.1955. The village of Gringley on the Hill is located about a mile from the canal and includes Beacon Hill with its commanding views. The church is mainly Gothic. In 1800, at the time of enclosure, the village was largely owned by the Duke of Rutland. *(NCCN000397)*

White Swan Inn, Drakeholes, c.1920. The inn is reflected in the water of the canal. It was owned by Thomas Parkinson in 1832 who also ran the wharf and the coal business.

The unusual design is due to

the owner of nearby Wiseton Hall who wanted it to blend in with his own building. Also nearby is the Drakeholes Tunnel which is only 134 yards long. *(NCCN002069)*

Drakeholes Basin, 19722. This used to be a very busy wharf. A coal merchant's business was run from here and it was also a staging place for coaches. Canal packet boats from Stockwith to Retford called at the wharf on Wednesdays and Saturdays. *Image credit: C.S. Brown (NCCN002014)*

Canalside, Wiseton, c.1900. The canal is seen surrounded by the former estate of Wiseton Hall. The present hall was built in 1962 and the village used to be part of the 3,800 acre estate. Originally owned by the Ackloms family the estate passed to the Earls Spencer and the Laycocks. Sir Robert Laycock decided the hall was too big and had it demolished in 1960. *(NTGM017930)*

Clayworth Bridge and Post Office, c.1910. The canal at this point is on the apex of a bend. The bridge was originally a swing bridge until it was rebuilt in 1890. The wharf had a regular packet boat which took produce to Retford market every day. Celery was a major crop and the Clayworth Pink was a well known variety. *(NCCN001965)*

View from Clayter's Bridge, Retford, 1905. The bridge is a replacement and carries the road from the town to North Leverton. It is also known as Spital Hill bridge. Close by was the town's workhouse built in 1838 to house two hundred people. The canal was once lined with boats as there was a brick and tile works located here. *(NCCN000593)*

Buildings between Clayter's Bridge and Grove Mill Bridge, 1982. This photograph shows the four storey building called Grove Street Mill. It was originally a malthouse but was converted to a flour mill at the turn of the century. The canal provided it with boiler fuel and grain which was turned into flour and transported to West Stockwith and beyond. The building was listed and saved in the 1980s.
Image credit: S.M. Cooke (NTGM017931)

Wesleyan Sunday School Trip at Grove Mill, 1906. This sight was a little unusual. Gas House Basin, as it was known was used by boats bringing cargoes for the mill and coal for the former gasworks nearby. The gasworks were built in 1831 and a 22 feet cast iron pillar holding five gas lamps was located outside the Town Hall. *(NCCN001416)*

The day the canal went down the plughole, 18th Aug 1978. The canal in this vicinity had become very dilapidated and needed a lot of dredging. During the work a chain was discovered and pulled. Unfortunately the whole canal between the surrounding locks was drained into the river. In the distance can be seen Gas House Bridge replaced in 1909 after a long argument between the canal owners and the town corporation. *(NCCN002341)*

Carolgate Bridge, 1968. This bridge has been widened a number of times leaving the original bridge underneath. This was once the Great North Road.

To the right of the photograph was where New Street Basin branched off. This could take 70 feet boats but nothing of the basin now remains. It was built by Taylor White and was purchased by the town in 1907. The area also boasted a brewery, a timber yard and a bone mill. *(NCCN000590)*

Corporation Wharf seen from Carolgate Bridge, c.1970. This was the commercial heart of Retford. There were a number of warehouses located here and a pair of stocks to punish any miscreants. The Corporation warehouse still survives with its bricked up windows and the remains of a crane. *(NCCN000701)*

Boat marina to the west of Carolgate Bridge, May 1971. The Corporation Wharf is now home to the Retford Mariners' Boat Club and originally boasted a dry dock. The warehouse has found a new life as a café. Nearby is the former Crown Inn, now the Litten Tree, which witnessed many of the meetings of the canal proprietors in the 1770s. *Image credit: S.J. Gostelow (NCCN000323)*

Corporation Lock, July 1968. This is the end of the broad section of the canal. It shows the former Navigation Inn which is now a private house. The warehouse was built by the Manchester, Sheffield and Lincolnshire Railway Company to try to prevent theft from the adjoining wharf. A toll office and a lock keeper's cottage were also located here. The chimney is part of Spicer's Mill. *(NCCN000592)*

Detail of Inkerman's or Iron Bridge, 1968. The original steps of the bridge can be seen here. From Town Lock the canal goes over three aqueducts including one over the River Idle. The canal passes a paper mill, founded in 1867, a wharf and a warehouse, before arriving at the bridge linking the town to the railway station. *(NCCN000702)*

Cemetery Bridge, 1911. The bridge is located close to the Girls' School and adjacent to the Victorian cemetery. The bend of the canal can be seen beneath the bridge. Nearby West Retford Hall was built in the early 1700s for the Huntsman family.
Image credit: Valentines (NCCN000947)

West Retford Lock, c.1960. Being close to West Retford Hall the canal is surrounded by high walls which were designed to stop intruders gaining access from the waterway. *(NCCN000916)*

West Retford Lock, 1968. West Retford Bridge often known as Woodcocks has been widened. There is a turning point which was used before the canal was finished. *(NCCN000884)*

Forest Lock. This is Forest Top Middle Lock and was the control point for the four locks named Forest. The lock keeper looked after this section of the canal and the locks to West Retford. He was also responsible for cutting the grass on the sides of the lock which would be boated along the canal. *(NCCN000707)*

Kilton Hill, 21st June 1963. Near Worksop timber yards imported timber from Norway and Sweden. Also nearby, Priorswell Brewery, of the Worksop and Retford Brewing Company, towered over the canal. *(NCCN000997)*

Court 2, Eastgate, 1953. In the background is Smith's Flour Mills, established in 1843. The building shown was built in 1906 and the wharf, located at the Mill, was used until 1947. *(NCCN001669)*

British Waterways Board Yard, Worksop, 1982. This is the control point for the waterway. The warehouse pictured can be seen straddling the canal. Boats used to moor underneath and goods were hoisted up to the upper floors. The warehouse was known as Pickfords from the company that traded here. *Image credit: S.M. Cooke. (NTGM017932)*

Straddle warehouse, c.1960. The warehouse still boasts the winding gear on the top floor but is now converted to a pub/restaurant. Worksop was changed by the coal industry from a sleepy town to a thriving one. The priory dates from the 12th century and the town is known as the 'Gateway to the Dukeries' due to there being many large estates in the area. *(NCCN001671)*

Woodend, Worksop, c.1960. At this point, near Rhodesia, the canal was culverted under the road. The section reopened for navigation in 2003. Rhodesia was built in the 1920s when the Shireoaks Colliery Company built houses for its new Steetley Colliery. The area is named after George Preston Rhodes who was chairman of the canal company. *(NCCN001653)*

Further Reading

General
Patrick, A, **'Canals in Nottinghamshire'**, Nottinghamshire County Council, 1975. An industrial archaeology survey.

Hadfield, Charles. **'The Canals of the East Midlands'**, David and Charles, 1970.

For thousands more images of old Nottinghamshire and its canals visit www.picturethepast.org.uk

Nottingham Canal
Chell, Bernard W, **'Nottingham Canal'**, ISBN 0 7524 3759 3, Tempus, 2006. A history and guide to the canal.

Zaleski, Stephen, **'The Nottingham Canal - Past & Present'**, ISBN 0 9519459 2 0, Local History Press, 2001. An illustrated history of the canal

Beeston Cut
see Chell, Bernard W

Grantham Canal
Cove-Smith, Chris, **'Grantham Canal Today: A brief history and guide'**, D Mitchell, 1974. An illustrated history and guide to the canal

See the Grantham Canal Society website, www.granthamcanal.com for more information

Chesterfield Canal
Richardson, Christine and Lower, John, **'Chesterfield Canal 2006-7'**, ISBN 978 0 9552609 0 2, Richlow Guides in 2007, A guide to the canal.

Roffey, James, **'The Chesterfield Canal'**, ISBN 0 86023 461 4, Barracuda Books, 1989. A history of the canal.

See the Chesterfield Canal Trust website, www.chesterfield-canal-trust.org.uk for more information

Acknowledgements

Acknowledgements are due to the Nottinghamshire County Council Libraries and Archives Publications Group, particularly Sam Collenette and Dorothy Ritchie. Thanks also to Christine Richardson, Chesterfield Canal Society and Mike Stone, Grantham Canal Society for their help; Nick Tomlinson, the team at Picture the Past, www.picturethepast.org.uk, and Nottinghamshire Archives staff for scanning and supplying digital copies of the images. Thanks for permission to use images are due to: Nottingham Central Library Local Studies Collection (NTGM picture the past references); Nottinghamshire County Council Libraries (NCC picture the past references); Nottingham City Council for permission to reproduce T.C. Moore's paintings; Derbyshire Museum and Art Gallery and Derbyshire Libraries; The Nottingham Evening Post Group; Lenton Local History Society; Stephen Best, Surrey Flying Services, Institution of Civil Engineers East Midlands; Martin Sentance for his permission to use F.W. Stevenson's photographs. Thanks also to the photographers: Reg Baker, R.G. Hughes, A.P. Knighton, Michael Payne, S.M. Cooke, C.M. Payne, Edwin Gordon, G.L. Roberts, Eric Lee, Ian Brown, S.J. Gostelow, G.A. Sewell, J. Orton, A. Johnson, A.W. Bourne, A.W. Bird, C.S. Brown, T.W. Wyncoll, Mr. Headland and all others who helped in the production and printing of this book.